WAYS THINGS MOVE

by Robin Nelson

first step nonfiction

Lerner Publications Company · Minneapolis

A **force** is a push or a pull.

Forces make things move in different ways.

Children walk in a
straight line.

A train moves in a straight line.

A crayon draws a
zigzag line.

Skiers make zigzag paths in
the snow.

A hoop spins in a **circle.**

A wheel moves in a circle.

A swing moves back
and forth.

A rocking chair moves
back and forth.

A toy car can move fast.

A bike can move fast.

A toy boat can move slowly.

A box is pushed slowly.

Everything moves with
a push.

Everything moves with a pull.

The Zigzag Street

There is a zigzag street in San Francisco, California. Some people call it the crooked street. The street goes down a very steep hill. The street was made with many short, sharp turns all the way to the bottom of the hill. The street was made like this so that cars would not go down the hill too fast.

Moving Facts

 A guitar string moves back and forth very rapidly when you pluck it. The string is vibrating. Vibrate means to move back and forth rapidly.

 A cheetah can run faster than any other animal on land.

 A snail is one of the slowest animals on land.

Race cars are driven on a track that is like a circle. In some races, the cars are driven around the track 200 times!

 Some animals run in a zigzag pattern to escape danger. Rabbits and deer run left and right to confuse whatever is chasing them. This also makes it hard to follow them.

Glossary

 circle – a round shape

 force – a push or a pull

 straight – no turns or curves

 zigzag – a line that goes one way then turns another way

Index

The photographs in this book are reproduced through the courtesy of: Digital Vision Royalty Free, cover, pp. 8, 12, 22 (top); © John Henley/CORBIS, p. 2; © Diane Meyer, p. 3; © Kwame Saikomo/SuperStock, pp. 4, 22 (second from bottom); © Richard Cummins, p. 5; © Todd Strand/Independent Picture Service, pp. 6, 15, 22 (second from top and bottom); Corbis Royalty Free, pp. 7, 13; Minneapolis Public Library, p. 9; Stockbyte Royalty Free, p. 10; © Ariel Skelley/CORBIS, p. 11; © Jane Sapinsky/CORBIS, p. 14; Brand X Pictures, p. 16; © Photodisc Royalty Free by Getty Images, p. 17; © Ron Watts/CORBIS, p. 18.

Lerner Publications Company
A division of Lerner Publishing Group
241 First Avenue North
Minneapolis, MN 55401 USA

Website address: www.lernerbooks.com

Library of Congress Cataloging-in-Publication Data

Nelson, Robin, 1971–
     Ways things move / by Robin Nelson.
         p.   cm. — (First step nonfiction)
     Includes index.
     Summary: Simple text introduces how different objects move, in different patterns and in different speeds, when pushed or pulled.
     ISBN: 0–8225–5136–5 (lib. bdg. : alk. paper)
     1. Force and energy—Juvenile literature. 2. Motion—Juvenile literature. [1. Force and energy. 2. Motion.]   I. Title.   II. Series.
QC73.4.N455   2004
531'.11—dc22   2003013890

Manufactured in the United States of America
1 2 3 4 5 6 – DP – 09 08 07 06 05 04